Introduction

I have decided to take the name of "Cilouete"
because I love the art form of silhouette and it
describes, in a way, all of my poems. The poems in
this book are my deepest, most heartfelt, most
intimate emotions and I would love to share with
all of those with the same love for the art of words
as I have. I have been writing since I was eight
years old. I have taken something so horrible and
turned it into a beautiful thing. I love the words my
pain has created and I am thankful for the gift that I
have been blessed with. I am thankful for all of you
that have taken the time to read my innermost
thoughts, desires, and emotions. I hope you enjoy
My Weeping Silhouette: Tale of a Few Tears as
much as I have enjoyed writing it.

"Motivation"

And on that night, I neglected to weep because I was taken there in my sleep and when I awoke, I saw your face in a completely different light in a completely different place. And on the next night, I neglected to weep to this gut wrenching song because I knew not that the lyrics were wrong. You were that person that I looked to with ease but you, oh but you, found a way for that to cease. As I lay to sleep that night, you were the product of my nightmares. I found myself scared of this person that I laughed with just yesterday. I couldn't even smile, I allowed you to take my joy away. And in that stage of life of mine, I'd say eight or nine, I knew nothing of the indecency roaming freely within humanity but you introduced it to me in the most inappropriate way. And as I grew, I never saw you as the bad guy and I didn't know why but a tear never fell from my innocent virgin eyes but I cried on the inside at night, unaware of my fear. And as time went on, I learned how much you were wrong and that this did not happen to every little girl and that this was not a part of playing house but I remained at the volume level of a mouse until I fell asleep. And my mother said I began to weep in the midnight hour but as I woke, my dreams were not even a memory and that baffled me. I was screaming to the audience with no ears, trying to get them to hear that I was hurting but I was in no pain because I couldn't allow them to see my face in that way..with tears on it. I couldn't put my finger on it but it hurt, just a little bit. It hurt more than a paper cut but not as bad as a bullet but it was going to be my secret but I was full of it. Thinking that this was okay. Thinking that this too will pass one day. Thinking that I was the reason for your dirty pleasing but I lied and one day, I cried, and to the closest person with an ear to hear, I acknowledged my past and then we wept in silence and my secret poems no longer had to be kept in silence. I could perform in rhymes my feelings to your violence and I don't hate you. I never have. You gave me the strength to not break when bent and I thank you for showing me that pain really is weakness leaving the body because now the thought of you does not bother me and you are my motivation to be a good mother, to be a successful writer, to be a story of a survivor versus that of a victim. So the tears I finally cried, I've just kicked them down to the place where all of my memories have gone and I smile as I create something else with the talent you have inspired. Thank you.

"You Hurt Me"

You hurt me...
And you didn't know because you weren't there
Last night as I was weeping.
You didn't see me with my blanket over my face
As if I were sleeping to hide the pain
From plain view and sight.
I cried last night
I wish we could be on the same page
And this was the same game that we'd played
And it was all a dream...
But you hurt me
And maybe I hurt you too
But I haven't the slightest clue
Because you weren't there to show me
The tears I imagine you had if I hurt you so bad
And I'm sorry
But you hurt me...
And you weren't there to pick up the pieces
I had to leave this on the corner of my pillow case
I had to be this strong suit in an empty place
I had to show strength in a broken place and it hurts
because you hurt me...
And this isn't even a poem
It's my pain that just so happens to rhyme
This is not a finger snapping event
Not this time because
You hurt me...
And it's been many days where I've applauded

An artists pain but I didn't know that it hurt so bad until
You hurt me...
Dear poets of expression, I've just learned a lesson
You take your tears and ball them up into words

For people to enjoy and listen as they snap
As you deploy your parachute of emotion as
You dive into this ocean of entertainment
I'm sorry for knowing that I smiled at your pain
Your talent was my gain but I had no idea until
You hurt me...-
I cried last night and you weren't there to dry my tears
Or even hear...why I was weeping when I should have
been sleeping because you left me as I cried as I died to
poetry of my own heart
Never again will I cry for this
As no tear is the same
I will pick myself up from this one day
As soon as I get the chance and opportunity
To tell you what you did to me
To tell you what you made of me
And I just can't believe it
You were supposed to love me like you said you did
but
You hurt me.

"My Idea"

See I-I had this idea
I had this plan where
I'd be your lady and
you'd be my man
and the world, ha,
it revolved around us.
See it stopped when we kissed
and it chilled when we hugged.
And the-the birds and bees they told
their story. And the waters made calm
just for you and me.
See I had this idea where a tear meant good
and you were the best thing walking
since candy houses in my neighborhood.
I had this vision in my mind that I was yours
and you were mine and that nothing could
break us apart not even time this time and
that I was your Bonnie and you were my Clyde
and we were each other's crimes.
I pictured in my mind that I was wifey that wifey
type that you liked and that it might actually be...
one day.
I had this idea that we were going to be together
no matter how much people thought it crazy.
I wasn't gonna be once, twice, but three times
a lady and maybe one day we would have a baby.
Then we would move into a big house with a picket
fence and a poodle...you know how that story goes.
And we were that couple that everybody knows and knew
and looked up to, envied, drew in there fairy tale story
books.
We were gonna vacate in a fancy state of mind

and lay with each other as I look into eyes and smile
as we make love with no penetration but rather dedication
to making these two hearts one.
See I-I had this idea
I had this plan where
I'd be your lady and
you'd be my man
and the world, ha,
it revolved around us.
See it stopped when we kissed
and it chilled when we hugged.
And the-the birds and bees they told
their story. And the waters made calm
just for you and me.
And I know that some ideas should just
remain ideas but I had to react and be proactive
and make this our reality.

"What Made Her Cry"

What do you do when the person you are is 'not who
everyone wants you be? What do you do when you get
tired of lying to yourself? What do you do when you
realize that you are not as happy as you know you should
be? Who do you call to talk to about the things that make
you cry? This is not who she wants to be and she's
lying...lying....lying to her self and her heart is telling her
no, telling her to let it go...telling her it's over. Over.
Reveal yourself, reveal yourself...open your eyes, try not to
cry as you look at the person that you've been hurting for
so long. She knows who she is but they don't want to see
her. They don't want to know her on the inside. They are
blissfully ignorant in their unknowing state of mind. She's

trying to find the time to say...all the things that make you cry. All the truths you thought were a lie...all the hopes you have to stop hoping for. All the dreams you have to wake up from. She wants to be who she is...let her be...love her wholeheartedly...hold her. Dry her heavy, sorrowful eyes as she reveals what made her cry.....she's afraid.

"A Life Always Remembered"

Sometimes, I still feel you in the midst of darkness, while the world is still asleep. Sometimes, I still hear your heartbeat playing a song for mine in the oddest of times...I know I can feel you inside, inside of me taking over like a child to his mother...clinging, living, loving, all from the inside. Sometimes, I feel that rush I used to get. While I'm lying awake in the broadest of day, alone, I feel your touch in the most innocent way. I curl up under my memories, under my promises...forever kept. My love, I hold you, with me, in my heart, in the deepest depths of my soul. You are just that, my soul, my world, my drive to push, to go, to live through you as you did me and one day, we'll have that eternity, that hug, that kiss a mother gives her child on a nights end. My love, my angel, my blood, my cries, my laughs, my tears, my joys...you are, me, that part of me that will live without a life, without a breath. Ones breathe that I can't give, I was your support through me, you lived, I love...still, you died, within my soul, solid proof withered away but you...you my love you live on in me for eternity. I can't hold you, but I told you, my love, I still feel you in the midst of darkness while the world is asleep. I hear you, my soul, a sound so passionate, so deep. The sound of a child's new, strong heartbeat....stopped...but forever going...through me....

A Life Always Remembered,

Mommy

"You Disappeared In Her Eyes Part I"

You disappeared in her eyes. She fell asleep holding you in her heart, comforted by the fact that you would be there with the morning but as the morning came her darkness fell as you walked away, dreams shot to hell. Images and visions, hopes, dreams, and wishes, became one of the unbecoming and she-she was lost. She searched above and beyond the lost and found, skies, seas, and grounds, her mind, her heart, her bed...she backtracked, thought back, stopped hands to head, mumbling indistinct passages of her brain and...nothing. You disappeared in her eyes. She painted this picture of you and saved a copy on her hard driven brain and penciled you in on her very motherboard. She traced your name in the foggy mirrors of her bathroom and defrosting windows of her car. She became what you wanted and you were her everything. She dreamt of you and smiled at your name got teary eyes talking about you and holding you the same. She went to sleep at night anxious about seeing you the next day so you two grown individuals could set out to play the way that you two did with poetic plans , what-if stories, and held hands. She curled up under your promises. She cuddled with your words. But she watched your flying angels turn into flipped birds. She cried out for you knowing that you'd changed that you were no longer her and him and nothing was the same. She read the words you left her in the emptiness of your bed telling her that she, like you, disappeared and that this exchange of lover's suicide note is not how you planned on spending the year. She sat in your face day to day with visions so unclear. You and her were not a "we". You had you and she had she and out of this a child was created...in your note, you bled a description of the little she. A product of a dying breed.

She cried for you. Begged for you to see her, to notice her, to love her, to be her...man...again. You pushed, she pulled, you fought, she fell, you closed your eyes, she closed her eyes and you both...disappeared. You, her, asleep, planning a life alone without the very heart of you. You walked away, she walked away. But wouldn't you know how that story ends...She came back...waiting for you...to open your eyes and see...ME!

"You Disappeared In Her Eyes Part II"

I waited. I waited for you to see....me and one day, you walked by and open your eyes...and smiled. I took a chance. I snuck a glimpse at the possibility of an "us" again but we were just...friends. The love for you had not faded and I was excited that we made it to a friendship before a relationship. Ha, Calm before the storm. I was prepared to forget, to forgive, to try..it...again. And we-we were happy. In your last note, you wrote of our child as "a product of a dying breed" but wouldn't you know we pushed and fought and continued to bleed the cries and attempts of a relationship. I loved you. I wanted you to love me like I loved you and fight for our family. But the more we fought, the more it brought us insanity. We made a move to start fresh but now there's nothing left but our product of the breed that we allowed to bleed until there was no blood to circulate through the veins of our attempts and...me. We tried, I tried, tell me you did because out of this last attempt, we produced another kid...a boy. One month shy of taking his first breath into a family that has nothing left but a mother and a sister and a father gone away. You disappeared...again. This time not just in my eyes but in her eyes and his eyes...but you're still Daddy, and I can't take that away from you but I cry one more time as I let my pearl go to sink to the bottom with no intentions of it being discovered or touching the surface again. I take with the memories of you being my boyfriend...in high school when it was...simple before we had responsibility because that's when you were nice to me. One last trip down memory lane. One last cry. One last smile before I close my eyes again and ...disappear.

"This"

This....is not MY life!
This...is not my destiny!
The usual 9 to 5, vacating to Wal-mart down the street,
is not for me.
I do not accept, check to check!
I will NOT be what statistics expect!
I live the dream life! I worry not!
I walk with sand between my toes,
under this sun...it's kind of hot!

 I am not the normal in a two bedroom, two bath
duplex that won't last.
I am not the cheeseburgers and French fries from Mickey
D's.
I do not wait for handouts. I do not beg please!

 I am that of victory!
I am that of success!
I am that of so much more
and I accept nothing less.

 I take care of my parents!
I smile when I say cheese!

 I believe in the miracles
that my God foresees!

 I am not a waitress at your local
seafood spot! I am successful
and I fall short not!

I am not content where my life sits
now! I will pray my prayer for these
walls to come down!

Behind these eyes, I hide the secret
miles, the secret laughs, the secret
stories of my present's past. I will be...
I AM one of my future.

I am not behind a desk. I am not in
your streets! I am not the dirty pimps
candy between his sheets!

I am not just successful! I am happy!
I am free! I am but I am all I plan to be.
One day in my future...one day very soon...

It'll be seen that I am on the move.
I had many chances that I blew away.
But my happiness, my kids happiness,
is the reason for this game.

We will vacate in the waterfalls any day we feel
because this 9 to 5 for a no man's check is not
where we stand still. Babies, I promise you.
I will be that of success so that we can be happy...
Don't ever take less!!!!!!

I refuse to lose! I refuse to settle! I refuse to sleep at night
before I win the battle! I refuse to not be happy and
content about life.

I am not one who's born to die...I am living to live... To live
passed day to day,

everyday retail, car sales, and pushing papers. I refuse to end this poem...the ending comes later....once we ALL smile!!!!!!!!!!!!

"I Used To Love Her"

I used to love her. This girl was so beautiful. This chick had it all together. She had the drive to go to the moon and back if you let her. Her face was so innocent, wrong wasn't in her nature little did we know we would grow to hate her. How could you hate such a beautiful girl, I'm not understanding. True enough she could be a little demanding and on the anxious side and times but who's not? Her head was on her shoulders not up her ass and she walked with dignity. I mean this girl had class. A selected few partners, didn't do drugs, finished high school, quick to hand out a hug but her fasaud became tainted, we see what she has painted, if only she had waited it wouldn't be known the thought of her selected few partners would quickly be thrown into a whirlwind of reality like it's beating the hell out me. Reality hit her causing the truth to seep out through her eyes and her mind caused the lies to trickle through her weapon of a tongue that she used. See her selected few partners became many. She allowed us all the pleasures of penetration in her mind. The mind that she played at the time. Her numbers quickly grew but remained a selected few...to you. She became a whore of the mind playing with hearts then innocent and confused. And there were drugs that she used quite frequently. The drug had an abbreviation of H-E-R and on Medicaid you could get M-E for a dollar if you qualify. See her class quickly got cancelled and this girl with a beautiful face could no longer be handled. And we all sit here in complete and utter disbelief with broken hearts and mixed emotions. We all went from trusting her to busting her up...in our sleep because who would dare harm such a beautiful face. I smile. As i chase myself, trying to catch the shadow I love to dance with because it catches my rhythm without any efforts. See you only know about a person what they tell you. And I might' a left out a few minor details about this female that proved to be important but if i advertised my ability to lie...Ha, I wouldn't get a boyfriend and couldn't sweet talk and cuddle with you and then your brother if i so choose. Now, I quickly became labeled with the N word. Yes, I mean nasty, naughty, not...a lady. Couldn't quite understand why I couldn't keep a man if I could easily buy you back. What does it mean to be independent? I think that's what my mother spoke of for 21 years but I mean come on now. Ya'll know how we work our ears. In one and...ha, yea. This time it might actually stick to my bones, still working on the brain because as long as i had cute face and my poetic side...i could make you love me. Until you hate me which seems to be inevitable. But i had my head on my shoulders and not up my ass and i walked with dignity, and i had class. Selected few partners, never did drugs, graduated high school always giving out hugs...and maybe a few rubs if you just let me. Well, damn, after kicking myself hard enough i began to see all this stuff. I did drugs. In fact i was addicted because i loved the way i felt when i ran through my own veins. I know insane right? I was my own drug. And i had class but I've just been expelled...for telling so many lies and making so many cry. RIP M-E. Rest in pieces not as a part of Jasmine. Now, lets have a moment of silence for her passing. And I know we shouldn't hate but im sure i can speak for us all when I say, we hated the girl with a beautiful face. But I ain't gonna lie.....I USED TO LOVE HER.

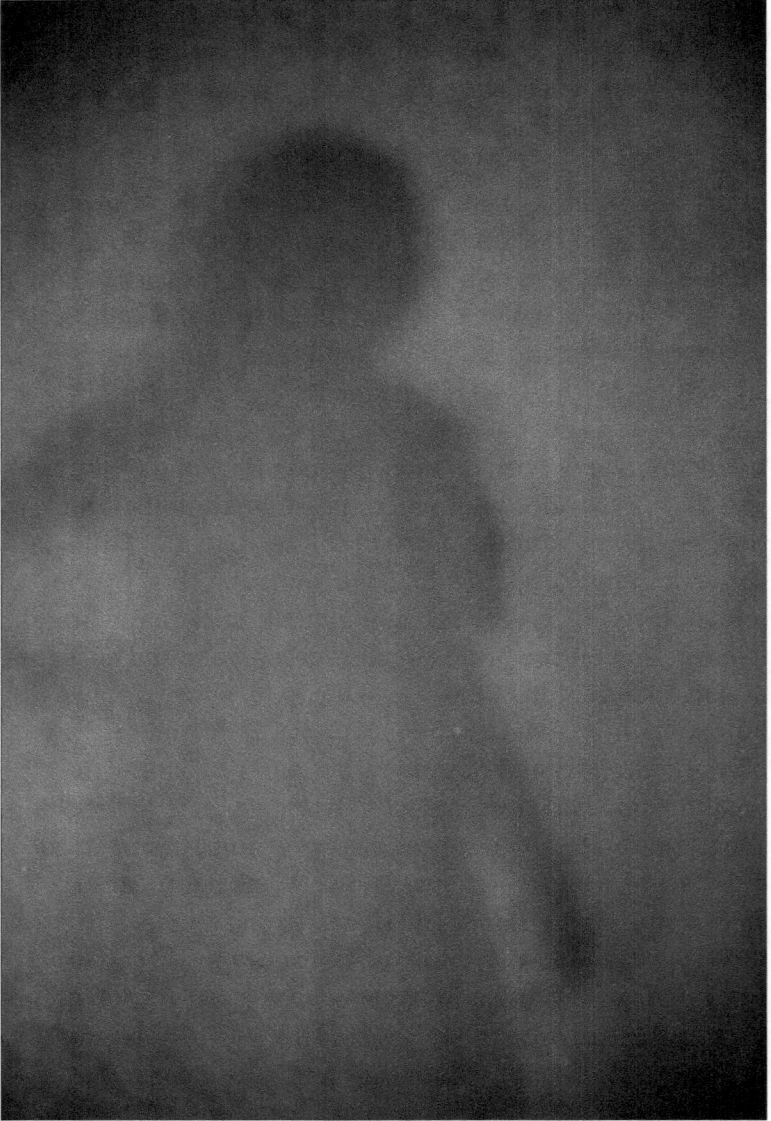

"My Life Story"

I don't want the struggle passed from my blood line.
I don't want to admit that the struggle is now mine.
I don't want to be the next ken to deal with the
principalities and abnormalities of leaving in this world.
I don't want to be known as a dead beat girl.

This, you see, is not just a poem. It is more than that.
It is a cry for help, a life's plea. A dream of ones future,
that one being me. It is a test of faith, a burden to my
dreams.
It is an obstacle to see if I can withstand the "how it
seems".
I am the youngest, eighteen years old. Living life, to MY
fullest. But oh, life is so cold. I see the ones before make
their mistakes. Life looks so fun from here, but those risks
I refuse to take. I'm twenty-one days shy of graduation,
closer to my life. Bills, stress, jobs, pain, maybe being
someone's wife.

But I refuse to be that one begging for a break. And I
refuse to be that one where aids, gangs, or drugs, is the
reason for my wake. I am on the road of making my
mother proud. I am doing the impossible; doing things you
thought weren't allowed. I am standing up, being me, the
me that everybody thought they'd never see.

I was quiet as a girl, I was in some serious pain. But I
REFUSE to let
that pain take me out this game. I have picked up on some
competitiveness and I'm determined to win, not just to say
I won but to prove that it could be done again. I won't
wake up in the mornings with tears running down my face.

I won't have a car full of clothes because I'm ready to change my place.
I won't have my kids crying to me, wondering how come they don't have friends because mommy and daddy can't stay in one spot to make any plans.

I will prove everybody wrong that said something bad on my name. I will show every one of them that I am not the same. I will protest against the fact that people can't change. And just because it's in your blood, that's how you gonna play the game. If that's the case, then I create my own game, my own rules, my own time, yes, I choose. I choose to make it, not to fake it, don't mistake it. Because even if I don't come out with everything topped. I will be the one to prove to you that this generational curse has STOPPED!!

I will make it; I'm determined to turn the table, to burn bridges that lead me to pain. Why, you want to know why, because that's how I play to win at this life's game.

This is not just a poem. These are not just words for me to get some glory. These, my dear readers, are the deepest thoughts and beginning words of my life story.

"Tomorrow Never Comes"

Tomorrow never comes,
it's stuck somewhere in the promises
of yesterday, even though yesterday was
over months ago. Yet and still you wait,
sleeping and waking, sleeping and waking,
your heart's constantly breaking in hopes that

tomorrow comes...but it never
does though you thought it would.
Dare you dream, dare you say, dare you think
that if I hold my breath, tomorrow will come and
save me because the promise of tomorrow is proven
to be true. I have even that much faith to say that
tomorrow is on its way and eventually my tomorrow
will become our today.

Sometimes, I even begin to see the first signs of
the rising sun to a new morning...then...no...it's
only a warning that time stops for no one and that
I should go on but I choose to hold on to the promise
of tomorrow. Even if tomorrow never comes, I'll hold
hold to the illusion of a new days rising sun.

It was told to me that you can't get to tomorrow
if you can't get passed today. But the memories
live in today and they're not going away.

There's a song in my soul, but I'm not sure I know the
lyrics.
It's too hard to explain, you'd just have to hear it.
It's almost like the sound of rain tapping into the waves of
an ocean. It makes your heart dance inside, though the
world can't see the motion. It's more on the lovers side,
you'd have to love to know. You'd have to stay to finish
the song, you can't let it go. Only one can here my song
and that's the mate to my soul.

"How Dare You"

How dare you...
confront my mistakes
try to push me 'til I break,
label me as fake!
How dare you...
let me go so
that I know that
it ain't me running
this show!

How dare you...
force me to move
when I was determined
not to lose when you showed
me that you owed me...nothing!
How dare you...
put a mirror in my face
to show me who was taking
your place, the cruel, deceitful,
mind inside of me!
How dare you...
show me that you cared for me,
and wanted the best for me,
and wouldn't give anything
close to less to me, and all
you did was love me!
How dare you...
make my cry by
saying goodbye to
someone that broke
your heart!
How dare you...
allow me to realize
that I'm living without you!

How dare you...
wait how dare I not say...
Thank You!

"My Used to Be's"

My used to be's were my everything but now the things
left to me are nothing. I'm empty, I've emptied the
contents of my life, laying it all bare, for me to share my
mishaps and flaws, to recap it all and show you what you
missed. The things that I broke I thought I fixed but I
tricked my mind, one more time, after another. I
uncovered the secret thoughts of a lover, one more time.
My thoughtless mind. I find the lies, I told with my eyes,
covering them with my sad story cries. Reality hit me. My
understandings get me. I came but you missed me. You
wonder is this me, the real me, with feelings? No, I'm
changing, I'm rearranging the order of my actions.
Changing the standards of my satisfaction. My used to be's
are too hard for you to see because it's my new reality.
With a smile on my face, I begin to chase dreams I didn't
dare to dream. But now I have the thing that motivates
me, that takes me and places me eye to eye with shame,
that IS pain. The reason for my used to be's that used to be
my everything until I emptied the contents of my heart.
Picking it apart. Ridding my life of what I broke twice just
to have a chance to speak of a romance that never existed
because I resisted and though it happened it was a
fantasy. Impossible for me to think it was reality. It's sad to
see this empty hole but I'm glad to set this lost soul free
and replace it, with me, without the used to be's because
I'm changing, rearranging my vision, I listened to the cries
of the people when they said "you hurt me...again. I
thought you were my friend." I apologize, that's no lie and
even if I never be claimed as your friend again I know my
life won't be just pretend with impressions because the

lesson taught by pain is a good one, I'm learning, I'm deserving of the commodities that come out of me. So when you ask me what I'm doing. Just know I'm changing for the better, so this will last forever. I'm getting it together. So who you will see will be without the used to be's. And though I appreciate your concern, I'm not changing for you...no...this is for me. No More Used To Be's!! Thank you.

"Heart of an Angel"

In the midst of darkness I see my regret. I have constant reminders...I
can never forget. I try to explain but they're all too upset at the fact that I did it and I can't take it back. I've gone against dreams that were once preset but these are the dreams that will never be met because in the broadest of day, my pain is revealed, no longer concealed but consumed I remain.
Losing at a pointless and forfeited game. It's not what you see because you see a shame. Disappointed at the girl you think I became, so you judge and hold a grudge, for who, when, and was. My desire burns like fire as I move higher on a scale of pain,
I want to change but emotionally I'm drained. I've been there and gone but you never knew I came...and you wait but it's late, it's over. There's no cover, no longer labeled as the lover nor the fighter but the liar with the fire and ability to burn your mind with timeless thoughts. Fighting fights that's already been fought and you continue to lose because you thought you were winning but you're beginning to see the ending of the mending of your broken heart and yet you still want to start and think you

can't be stopped but in a matter of seconds you will be dropped by pride all jokes aside. You can't just let it ride nor can
you hide from reflections of you in your own eyes because eyes will not lie and you can't make them cry if they're dry. End your search of sympathy and acknowledge me despite my mistakes,
my stupidity. See me for me. I apologize, sincerely, if you can hear me but it's my last time, my last bit of effort. I see your pain, my lies, the hurt, but I sit here alert, aware of my
surroundings though I'm drowning in judgment. How could I love this? I have no choice but to live this don't give this a bad name. Though I've made mistakes and I have plenty of regrets,
still I believe in the midst of my wrong my heart is still the home of an angel.

"My Apologies"

Victimized by all the lies, the viscous crimes,
deceitful eyes, but only, I'm not the victim,
more like the villain doing all the killing, not
of souls but love, hope, and feelings, plus dreams
that I've seen for myself but I've allowed to wither
away at the end of the day while the world rested
I invested in the pain I inflicted when I flipped it and
reversed it as though I rehearsed it with characters and
a script it was a trip until I got hit and dropped to my knees
watching my soul escape through my veins I bleed I need...
you to come through like I didn't do for you but please as I
lie here on my knees begging for my last since I gave up

my world for a baby and a girl I have nothing...not even that and for such reasons I cannot go back so I feel victimized by my lies, my viscous crimes that I've committed against you making the
words "I do" meaningless to the world but meaning the world to me. I feel so low, so lost, so alone, because now I'm actually lonely without you to hold me. I felt like I was on top of the world but I was dropped my world was rocked, the time has stopped...
I cry because what I want but I know I cannot have. Do I know that it's now my past, a past that I cannot relieve. Oh what I would give to love you again and you the same. But because of my lies, I guess it means nothing for me to say "I apologize". But I really do and I love you.

"Your Main"

I don't want to be your main babe,
I want to be your only.
I don't always want sex,
Sometimes you should just hold me.
I don't want to compete with the girls with no face.
I don't want you to let someone else take my place.
Every relationship has its problems...but I have my pen and
my paper and I'm ready to solve them. If I need to break
out the calculator, be that then. But I'm not gonna pretend
like I'm okay with you having a possible side chick when I
should be your side, front, back, and in between. Maybe
you don't know what I mean when I say I love you. I love
you means I'm willing to fight for a relationship with
potential so if this is the end for us, class can be let out for
early dismissal. I won't be stuck on stupid but I'll work for
something worth the pain. I'm not going to inflict
unnecessary wounds on myself or let you drive me insane.
Believe you me, I pray we make it. But if I'm just your
"Main" I'm not going to take it.
I don't want to be your main babe,
I want to be your only,
And if you want me to be your anything
You're gonna have to show me.
I'm young but I'm not dumb. I am subject
To the possibility of heartbreak but I knew
That when I enrolled in your class for you to teach me
And show me how well you could love me and hold me.
Don't make me out to be the bad guy when I say
I refuse to be used, to be second because even
If I am your main, I'm not you're only lady.
And I refuse boo, I just refuse to allow you to play me.
So tell me now, if you want me or me and other women

because you very well may be able to walk and chew gum
at the same time. But you're not gonna waste my time.
I didn't think you were that kind and I really thought you
Were mine. Maybe I'm overreacting, maybe what you
Were saying and what I was saying was exactly the same.
But I'm not gonna be your girl, If I'm gonna be your main.
HEART OF HEARTS SAYS NO.

"Oh Well, I'll Write About It"

You hurt my feelings...
but I'm a grown woman so
I just won't cry about it.
I guess I could just write about it
and pretend like there's nothing to
deny about it. I'll just lie about it!

But man, it sort of hurts but
I'm a mommy and I can't show
pain in front of my pupils and I can't
let it rain on me because it just might
confused them so I'll be superwoman.
I'll be the woman that feels nothing but
the pen in her hand and tears in her throat.
With a story to share in a heartbroken note
but I can't cry. I can't show that emotion,
no, not that emotion, not that pain..not that one
because the last time I checked, it was wrong to cry.

What was it Fergie? Big Girls Don't Cry.
But I don't want to be a big girl because it hurts.
I guess I'll put my training pants on, I'm a big
girl now. I can't just shout it out. I can't just cry about it.

I'm a grown up. I'm a mommy now.
Oh well, I'll just write about it.

You are my talent, you are the reason
for my skill. You pay the bills that cost nothing

but my tears. Every time you hurt me, I create
a masterpiece. Every time you leave me, I stitch
up a bleeding speech. I should be happy huh? I should
be grateful that you're so mean and ignorant and blind
to my opinion. I should shake the hand of the man that
for being the reason for my riches...before the riches but
it sounds good.

I'll look weak in your eyes
if I allow my eyes to show
your eyes that they can cry
because of what you said.
Last I checked, my body wasn't dead
so I can't cry about it. I guess I could just
write about it and read it to you and leave
the bleeding to you as my words are the dagger
you're holding to your own heart with no control
because you hurt my feelings so you've pierced your own
soul when you saw the success of the one you betrayed
when you played the forbidden game in Eden's garden.
You demand I cry well I beg your pardon.
I'll never let you know that I did once cry about it.
But I will let you see that I did just write about it...

And now I smile.

"Victoria's Little Secret"

Last I checked, my name was not Victoria
and I wasn't giving away my secret.
I made a promise to my promise that I
would always keep it. I mean it when I
leave it bleedin' on the pages of my diary.
Fire me, sue me, hate me, accuse me but you
will never know me or my secret. You cannot
upset me, protect me from you wrath. You
cannot take from my tomorrow because I gave
you your passed. I'm finished with the business
you told me to mind. I am walking away. You lose
this time. I am not your screw up. I am not your mistake.
I am not the forbidden fruit you claim you never ate.
I am a promise to my promise that you will never
win again. Best wishes, all the luck with you, I send. But
you, my dear, are not a friend of mine so step behind and
watch a miracle bloom. You are now fed with a tarnished
silver spoon that I dropped in the dirt and neglected to
rinse off because you just picked the right one to piss off.
And considering the circumstance, you've gotten of easily.
I'm letting you walk away with dignity, silly me, so
pleasantly, take your baby lies and crying eyes and drown
them in your tears. And cry a river to the ocean because
you no longer have my ears.
Because last I checked, my name was not Victoria but
here's another secret for ya. You are not my factor. I no
longer need the pen, paper, or Google to figure you out
because the secrets out...at the cost of your being. Good
seeing the one who no longer has a meaning. Demeaning?
Precious. God bless us, you need it because I just let you in
on Victoria's little secret....

You Lose!

"The Deepest Love"

It's kind of like innocent until proven guilty...not in the way that a man doesn't deserve to be treated as a man should by his woman but in the sense of you will have to earn that deepest love I possess. I don't want to fall in love with a man. I do not want to fall for you. I want you to take my hand, look me in my eyes, and walk...with me into love. A woman should not love every man that she has fallen for like she loves her husband. As hard as I love and as much as I give when I do give my heart to a person, I am careful to hold back bits and pieces of that deepest love I possess. It kills me a little bit more inside to know that I have given my soul to a man that was not, is not, will not be, my husband and he gave it back. I give that love with a no return policy and somehow he found a way to give it back to me after he shared it with his indecency and broke me in places that were never meant to bend. I can't pretend that you will have all of me when I know it's not a possibility unless you can show me. Never promise me a promise that you promise not to break because sometimes they fall with words and shatter beyond repair and though you may have cared and tried with all of your being to not break it...something with the power to shake it could take it and abuse it and mistake it as...love. I'm not sixteen anymore. I love you means more to me that a trip to the movie theater last Saturday and a teddy bear with the year on the foot. I love you means holding hands and having fun to the point of which we reach the top of our hill and when we take that inevitable fall, we, still hand in hand, climb back up to the top on the windiest, rainiest, earth shattering day of the year. And as we stand at the top of that hill with weak knees and sweating brow we turn to each other, exhale, and know that we have climbed our trials together and we withstood disagreement, temptation, irritation, selfishness, loneliness, money matters, family matters, blood, fights, and tears and we STILL love each other. That is what love means to me. So if your knees can withstand a couple of hills then I digress and give to you the deepest love that I possess.

www.ingramcontent.com/pod-product-compliance
Lightning Source LLC
Chambersburg PA
CBHW051713090426
42736CB00013B/2686